THEMATIC UNIT
BIRDS

D1408611

Written by Barbara Hollis

Teacher Created Materials, Inc.
6421 Industry Way
Westminster, CA 92683
www.teachercreated.com
©1992 Teacher Created Materials, Inc.
Reprinted, 2000
Made in U.S.A.
ISBN-1-55734-256-3

Edited by
Karen Goldfluss
Illustrated by
Keith Vasconcelles

Table of Contents

Introduction

Birds contains a captivating whole language, thematic unit. Its 80 exciting pages are filled with a wide variety of lesson ideas and reproducible pages designed for use with primary children. At its core are two high-quality children's literature selections, *Feathers for Lunch* and *Chicken Little*. For these books, activities are included which set the stage for reading, encourage the enjoyment of the book and extend the concepts gained. In addition, the theme is connected to the curriculum with activities in language arts (including daily writing suggestions), math, science, social studies, art, music, and life skills (physical education, cooking, etc.). Many of these activities encourage cooperative learning. Suggestions and patterns for bulletin boards and unit management tools are additional time savers for the busy teacher. Furthermore, directions for student-created Big Books and a culminating activity, which allow students to synthesize their knowledge in order to produce products that can be shared beyond the classroom, highlight this very complete teacher resource.

This thematic unit includes:

- **literature selections**—summaries of two children's books with related lessons (complete with reproducible pages) that cross the curriculum

- **poetry**—suggested selections and lessons enabling students to write and publish their own works

- **planning guides**—suggestions for sequencing lessons each day of the unit

- **writing ideas**—daily suggestions as well as writing activities across the curriculum, including Big Books

- **bulletin board ideas**—suggestions and plans for student-created and/or interactive bulletin boards

- **curriculum connections**—in language arts, math, science, social studies, art, music, and life skills such as cooking, physical education, and career awareness

- **group projects**—to foster cooperative learning

- **a culminating activity**—which requires students to synthesize their learning to produce a product or engage in an activity that can be shared with others

- **a bibliography**—suggesting additional literature and nonfiction books based on the theme

> To keep this valuable resource intact so that it can be used year after year, you may wish to punch holes in the pages and store them in a three-ring binder.

Introduction *(cont.)*

Why Whole Language?

A whole language approach involves children in using all modes of communication: reading, writing, listening, observing, illustrating, experiencing and doing. Communication skills are interconnected and integrated into lessons that emphasize the whole of language rather than isolating its parts. The lessons revolve around selected literature. Reading is not taught as a separate subject from writing and spelling, for example. A child reads, writes (spelling appropriately for his/her level), speaks, listens, etc. in response to a literature experience introduced by the teacher. In this way, language skills grow naturally, stimulated by involvement and interest in the topic at hand.

Why Thematic Planning?

One very useful tool for implementing an integrated whole language program is thematic planning. By choosing a theme with correlating literature selections for a unit of study, a teacher can plan activities throughout the day that lead to a cohesive, in-depth study of the topic. Students will be practicing and applying their skills in meaningful contexts. Consequently, they tend to learn and retain more. Both teachers and students will be freed from a day that is broken into unrelated segments of isolated drill and practice.

Why Cooperative Learning?

Besides academic skills and content, students need to learn social skills. No longer can this area of development be taken for granted. Students must learn to work cooperatively in groups in order to function well in modern society. Group activities should be a regular part of school life and teachers should consciously include social objectives as well as academic objectives in their planning. For example, a group working together to write a report may need to select a leader. The teacher should make clear to the students and monitor the qualities of good leader-follower group interactions just as he/she would state and monitor the academic goals of the project.

Why Big Books?

An excellent cooperative, whole language activity is the production of Big Books. Groups of students, or the whole class, can apply their language skills, content knowledge, and creativity to produce a Big Book that can become a part of the classroom library to be read and reread. These books make excellent culminating projects for sharing with parents, librarians, other classes, etc. Big Books can be produced in many ways and this thematic unit includes directions for at least one method you may choose.

Feathers for Lunch

by Lois Ehlert

Summary

Acclaimed artist Lois Ehlert gives us another innovative teaching book with vibrant, dramatic colors. A playful but hungry cat is loose in the garden filled with breathtaking, colorful birds and plants. Children anticipate whether or not the bird will feast this day. Meanwhile they are meeting twelve common birds and learning to identify each one. There is also a detailed glossary at the back of the book sure to please any budding bird watcher.

The outline below is a suggested plan for using the various activities that are presented in this unit. You may adapt these ideas to fit your own classroom situation.

Sample Plan

Lesson 1

- Prepare Bird Folders (page 6).
- Brainstorm "What We Know About Birds" (page 6).
- Read *Feathers for Lunch*.
- Color and sort bird pictures (page 7).
- Send home parent letter (page 73).

Lesson 2

- Begin a Word Bank (page 45).
- Share items students bring in (page 6).
- Introduce Bird Sightings (page 7).
- Reread *Feathers for Lunch*.
- Begin Bird Watch/Incubator Observations Diary (page 7).

Lesson 3

- Do Egg Graphs (pages 18-19).
- Develop pocket chart story (page 7).
- Continue diary entries.

Lesson 4

- Complete Punctuation Peck (page 46).
- Choose a Bird Art activity from page 16.
- Add facts to "What We Know About Birds" (page 6).
- Examine eggs with A Look Inside An Egg (page 20).
- Continue diary entries.

Lesson 5

- Learn about and write cinquains (pages 41-42).
- Play Put the Hen in the Henhouse (page 51).
- Do Birds of a Feather Flock Together (pages 21-22).

Lesson 6

- Study and write about owls (page 9).
- Do Owl Tear Art (page 69).
- Make a Big Book (page 50).
- Continue diary entries.

Lesson 7

- Research birds and complete All About Birds (page 8).
- Write an innovation (page 8).
- Create An Egghead (page 65).
- Continue diary entries.

Lesson 8

- Play Birdwalk Relays and Red Robin (page 63).
- Share student reports.
- Make Nibble Nests (page 70).
- Make bird feeders using Buffet for Birds (page 57).

Overview of Activities

SETTING THE STAGE

1. Prepare the classroom for a Bird Unit. Assemble a bulletin board following the directions and patterns on pages 76 and 77. Create a Learning Center and displays using suggestions on page 74. (Include both fiction and nonfiction books in the center.) Send home a letter to parents announcing the start of the unit and requesting materials (page 73).

2. Contact a local Audubon Society for guest speakers and information.

3. Divide a large piece of butcher paper in half and display. Label one half "Things We Already Know About Birds." Brainstorm with students what they know about birds and list ideas on butcher paper. Label the second half of the paper "What We've Learned About Birds." Explain that information will be added to this section as the unit progresses.

4. Make copies of the Bird Folder cover (page 10) and distribute it to students. Have each student fold a 12" x 18" (30cm x 45cm) piece of construction paper in half to make a folder. Glue the cover onto the folder. Explain that it will be used for collecting materials and ideas, and for storing activity pages from the unit. Materials compiled in the folder could be used as part of a portfolio assessment. See *Portfolio Assessment* (TCM #145) for ideas on using portfolios in the classroom. If possible, laminate folders for durability.

This Bird Folder belongs to

_____

5. Show students the cover of *Feathers for Lunch*. Ask them what the title might mean. List student ideas. Refer back to these for comparison after reading the story.

6. Plan ways to attract birds to a spot in your school yard. Decide which methods would be most successful and/or practical. (*Bird* by David Burnie, provides excellent information and illustrations.) Make Bird Feeders (page 57).

7. Share with the class any bird nests, feathers, and/or artifacts at your disposal. Encourage them to bring in any bird related items they may have. Students can tell about the items and where they acquired each, as well as other pertinent information.

   If possible, keep these on display for observation and reference in a Curiosity Corner or at the Learning Center.

8. The unit comes to life when you hatch chicks. Make an incubator (see instructions on page 59). Commercial incubators can be purchased through school supply catalogs. Fertile eggs can be obtained from professional hatcheries or people in your community.

9. Word Banks are created by students for students. Display a Bird Word Bank using suggestions on page 45. Students can add to the list throughout the unit, especially for writing activities.

Overview of Activities *(cont.)*

ENJOYING THE BOOK

1. As you read this book aloud make sure you allow children time to enjoy the beautiful art work on each page. Also, pause as you come to an obvious rhyme so students can complete the pattern. (Tell children the actual names of birds and plants on each page the second time you read the book.)

2. For recall and comprehension, ask the following questions: What birds were in the story? What plants were in the story? What places? Where did the cat go to try to get birds? What sound did the cat always make? Why? What sounds did the birds make?

3. Have children color and cut out the 12 birds introduced in this book (pages 11-13). Sort them by color, size, beak shape, feather structure, or other features that will help familiarize students with their feathered friends. For durability, glue them onto index cards. Put the name of the bird on the back of the card. Students can use the pictures as flashcards. Pairs of students could play "Memory" or "Concentration" by using 2 sets of cards. (Cover bird names first!)

   Practice listening and oral language skills by having students describe a bird to a partner. Using the descriptions and picture cards, the partner must try to guess the bird.

4. Look at the birds from the story, *Feathers for Lunch*, and decide which birds may be in your area. Take the class for a bird walk, having students use page 15 to record bird sightings. The information gathered can be used to complete Bird Watch Diary entries (page 17). File pages in student made bird folders (page 10). Use diaries periodically. Encourage students to keep track of bird sightings outside of school as well.

5. Pocket charts are a valuable tool for providing shared experiences. Reproduce the word strips (page 14) onto construction paper and laminate, if possible. For flannel boards, glue pieces of felt or sandpaper to the back of word strips. Self-stick magnetic strips (available in craft stores) can be attached to word strips for use on magnetic boards.

   Select various bird pictures from pages 11-13 to complete the story. Ask students to give a physical description of each bird. Discuss where it lives and what it eats, and relate it to the text and illustrations from the book.

6. Using the text, review with students the general locations of birds from *Feathers for Lunch*. Then do Birds of a Feather Flock Together (pages 21-22).

7. Have fun graphing with Egg Graphs (pages 18-19). Tally how many of your students are egg eaters. Invite students to taste and choose the type of egg preparation they prefer and graph the results.

Overview of Activities *(cont.)*

ENJOYING THE BOOK (cont.)

8. A Look Inside An Egg (page 20) provides a hands on science experience that will stir everyone's interest. Students can work in small groups and discuss their observations. Compare each group's ideas.

9. If you have set up an incubator (page 59) use a format similar to that on page 17 to keep a diary of activity within the incubator. Set aside time for daily student observations and class discussion.

10. Have students prepare a Bird Facts worksheet (page 40). Include birds introduced in the unit and those of special interest to students, such as our national bird, the bald eagle. (Mighty Eagle, on page 61, provides teacher background information and suggested activities.) The Bird Facts worksheet can be used as part of daily writing (page 39).

EXTENDING THE BOOK

1. Make a Big Book. Use the sentence strips from page 14 (or create your own) and follow directions on page 50.

2. Play Put the Hen in the Henhouse game (page 51). Students can learn game strategies while working cooperatively. Geoboards may be used.

3. Use some of the Bird Art ideas on page 16.

4. List common features of all birds, using Attributes of Birds (page 54). Reproduce the page for students to keep in folders and use as a reference, or display a chart of attributes in the classroom.

5. Have students research birds. Use All About Birds (page 23), the Word Bank, Attributes of Birds (page 54), Learning Center materials, and as many other resources as possible to assist students. Share completed reports.

6. Discuss how some birds have become extinct and find out which birds are now protected by law. Use bird stationery, page 75. Write for the endangered and threatened species list:

   The Office of Endangered Species
   U.S. Fish and Wildlife Service
   Washington, D.C. 20240

7. Write an innovation. An innovation is the creation of a new text from existing stories, books, or poems, by substituting content to fit a new story. *Feathers for Lunch* could become *Fishhooks for Dinner* and might tell about a fisherman whose catch gets away.

   Model an innovation for the class. Then write one together (as a class project) and display it, or encourage students to develop their own stories.

8. Reinforce the mechanics of writing with Punctuation Peck (page 46). This may be done in cooperative groups or individually. Discuss the corrections and punctuation rules which apply.

8

Overview of Activities *(cont.)*

9. Use pages 41-42 to introduce the poetic form of the cinquain. Model a word cinquain with the class. Students can use the suggestions and frame on these pages to help them develop their own cinquains. Completed cinquains could be mounted inside colorful egg shapes and arranged in a large nest background for display.

10. Show and discuss books about owls (bibliography, page 79). Discuss unique features of owls (usually nocturnal, keen eyesight, distinct eye structure). Be sure to have books about owls in the Learning Center. Distribute The Amazing Owl Report (page 44) form to students. Allow adequate time for reading and completing a report. When students are done, have them share their discoveries with the class.

11. Make Owl Tear Art on page 69, using the following materials: brown grocery bags; scissors; glue; 9" x 12" (23 cm x 30 cm) brown construction paper (enough for class). Duplicate the pattern on page 69 onto brown construction paper and have students cut out the pattern. Tear up brown bags into quarter size pieces. Glue the torn pieces in layers onto the owl shape. Cut out the eyes and beak and glue on.

    Completed owls can be used as borders for room displays and to accompany projects and writing activities. (Create a "Wise Owl" sayings bulletin board with student ideas on wise decision making rules. Other titles could be "A Word to the Wise" or "Words of Wisdom.")

12. Class books can be made from student reports. Display proudly in an area of the classroom for others to enjoy.

13. Set up a bird feeding station around the school. Use Buffet for Birds (page 57) to build various types of feeders. Encourage students to bring in some of the materials. Use the station to attract and watch birds as often as possible. Record observations in daily diaries.

14. Prepare and enjoy Nibble Nests (page 70). Students can work in groups to mix ingredients for a delicious snack. You may wish to prepare these treats as part of the culminating activity (page 71).

15. How and where do birds build nests? What materials do they use? What types of nests are there? Discuss these questions. *Bird,* by David Burnie, provides excellent photographs and information on nest building. Do Building a Nest (page 60) and ask students to color and sequence the pictures. Students could make Brown Bag Nests (page 16) at this point if they have not already done so.

16. Provide students with copies of Create an Egghead (page 65) and encourage them to use their imaginations in designing a variety of eggheads. Challenge them to express emotion through facial expressions on some of the eggs.

This Bird Folder belongs to

_____

10

*Use with activity 3, page 7. See answer key (page 80) for bird card names.

Feathers for Lunch

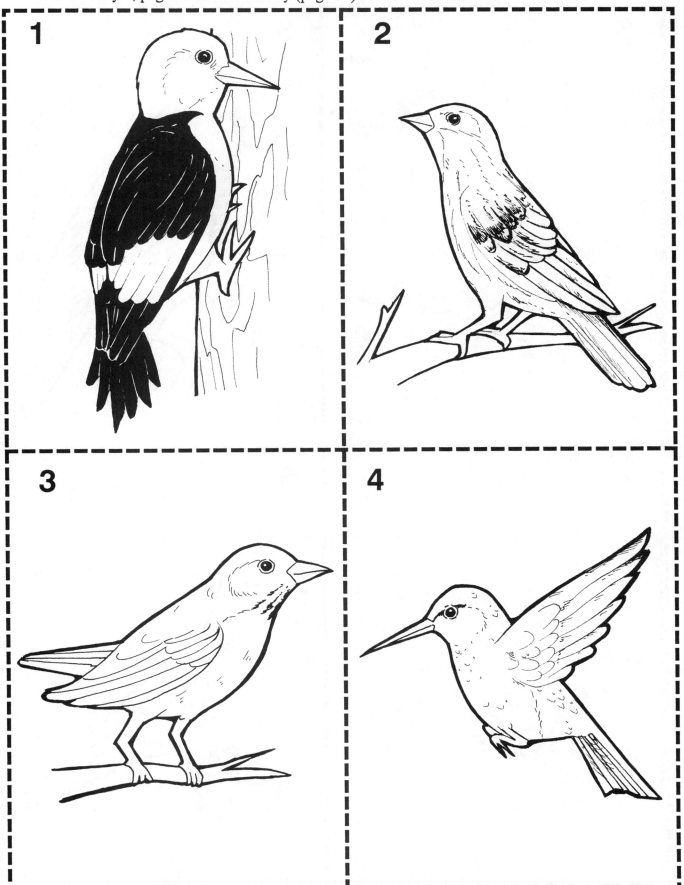

11

*Use with activity 3, page 7. See answer key (page 80) for bird card names.

Feathers for Lunch

Pocket Chart Strips

Pop!

An egg cracks!

Out comes a

Use the word strips above with activity 5 on page 7.

14

Bird Sightings

Name: _____ Date:_____

I predict I will see_____birds today.

I saw:

Tally	Bird	Tally	Bird
☐	American Robin	☐	Red-headed Woodpecker
☐	Blue Jay	☐	Red-winged Blackbird
☐	Northern Cardinal	☐	Mourning Dove
☐	House Wren	☐	Ruby-throated Hummingbird
☐	Northern Oriole	☐	House Sparrow
☐	Northern Flicker	☐	American Goldfinch
☐	Other _____	☐	Other _____

I saw_____birds today.

Bird Art

Feather Painting

Materials: foam meat trays or paper plates; diluted tempera paint (colors of your choice); feathers (purchased from a craft store); white construction paper

Directions:

Pour paint into trays or plates.

Dip feathers into paint tray.

Brush across construction paper.

Repeat for desired effect. (More than one color may be used to create interesting designs.)

Feather painting can be used to border poems and stories. Or, laminate paintings and use as background material for student bulletin board displays.

Birdwatch Binoculars

Materials: bathroom tissue paper tubes (2 per student); tempera paint; yarn; hole punch; glue or tape

Directions:

Children glue or tape two tubes together; then paint the outside. When thoroughly dry, attach yarn by punching a hole on the outside of the tube ends (same end of each). The yarn serves as a neck strap. Your class can bird watch to their hearts delight.

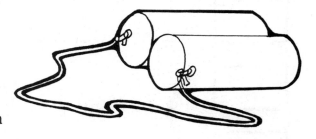

Brown Bag Nests

Students will enjoy making their own nests. After discussing the kinds of materials birds use to construct a nest, prepare a student-generated list of items that birds might use from their surroundings. Encourage students to bring these in to use as nesting supplies.

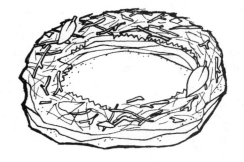

Materials: brown paper sandwich bags (1 per student); glue; nesting materials

Directions: Have students fold in the top edges all the way around the bag with both hands and roll inward. Keep rolling the edges down until they reach the bottom of the bag. Press the rim down to flatten it a little. The rim of the nest should look irregular to give it a more natural appearance.

Glue nesting materials all around the rim. Completed nests provide a decorative 3-D addition to student displays. Or, use the nests to harbor plastic pop-apart eggs. The inside of the nest could also be used for bean counting and estimation activities in math.

Name _____

Bird Watch Diary

Use this diary to keep a record in your folder of how many birds you see each day of birdwatching. Tell about and draw pictures of them. Watch your bird diary grow!

Day_____Date_____ Tally of birds I saw: [ ] One bird looked like: _____ _____ Draw.	Day_____Date_____ Tally of birds I saw: [ ] One bird looked like: _____ _____ Draw.
Day_____Date_____ Tally of birds I saw: [ ] One bird looked like: _____ _____ Draw.	Day_____Date_____ Tally of birds I saw: [ ] One bird looked like: _____ _____ Draw.

Egg Graphs

Students will enjoy giving their input on egg preferences while making the following class pictographs.

Making An "Egg"cellent Choice

Directions: Copy the chart below onto butcher paper. Cut out egg shapes (enough for the entire class) from white and blue pieces of construction paper. Be sure that if you have 30 students, 30 eggs would fit into one of the chart categories. Assign white eggs to the "Likes Eggs" category and blue to the "Doesn't Like Eggs" box. Have each student choose the egg color that reflects his/her preference and glue it onto butcher paper. Count and discuss results.

Making an "Egg"cellent Choice	
Likes Eggs	**Doesn't Like Eggs**

What Will I Have for Br"egg"fast Today?

Try the following egg tasting activity to determine which egg preparation students enjoy most.

Preparation: Provide a table with paper plates, plastic forks, and samples of different egg preparations (scrambled, fried, hard boiled, deviled). Allow students to sample a small amount of each and choose a favorite. (Check for possible food allergies before tasting.)

Use a large piece of white construction or butcher paper to duplicate the chart below. Be sure chart columns are large enough to accommodate vertical rows of squares from page 19. Make copies of egg picture squares and cut them out. Place the pictures in front of the matching foods at the table. When students have sampled eggs and selected a favorite, have them glue or tape the squares to the chart in the appropriate columns. (They may color pictures first.) Those who have no favorite (dislike or cannot eat eggs) should use the "no way" column. When the activity is completed, tally and discuss results. Emphasize the value of graphs in providing instant visualization and comparison of data.

What Will I Have for Br "egg" fast Today?				
Scrambled	Fried	Hard Boiled	Deviled	No-Way

Egg Graphs *(cont.)*

Use the picture squares below to complete the egg tasting activity on page 18.

Note to teacher: Make enough copies so children may choose their favorite.

Name_____

A Look Inside An Egg

Do you know what the inside of a chicken egg looks like? Can you guess how many parts it has?

I think a chicken egg has_____parts.

Use these materials to check your answer:

a raw egg   waxed paper   paper towels (for clean up)

Directions:

1. Put a raw egg on top of a large sheet of waxed paper. Look at it closely.
2. When you are finished looking at the outside of the egg, carefully break the egg. Try not to break the yolk.
3. Look carefully at what is on the waxed paper.
   Use a pencil or your finger to touch the different parts. Count the different parts. Draw what you see.

Results and Conclusions:

1. How many egg parts did you see?

   _____

2. Is the number more, less, or the same as what you thought?

   _____

3. What did you learn? Can you name the egg parts?

   _____

   _____

Name _____

Birds of a Feather Flock Together

Directions: Use the map below to show some of the places where the birds from the story live. Your teacher will explain how to fill in the map.

Birds of a Feather Flock Together
(cont.)

Teacher Directions: Discuss the meaning of the phrase "birds of a feather flock together." Why do you think a type of bird may be able to live in one place and not in another?

Duplicate the map on page 21 and the chart below for each student. Use the map to review directions north, south, east, and west. Next, discuss where birds from *Feathers for Lunch* live, using information from the chart below.

Help students locate the areas where different species live and write the bird's corresponding number on the map. Then they may color the map and attach the chart as a key.

Number	Bird Name	Where It Lives	Number	Bird Name	Where It Lives
1	American Robin	Throughout the United States and Canada	7	Northern Oriole	Throughout the United States and Canada
2	Bluejay	Eastern United States and central and eastern Canada	8	Mourning Dove	Throughout the United States and southern Canada
3	Northern Cardinal	Eastern United States, Arizona	9	Northern Flicker	Throughout the United States and Canada
4	Ruby-throated Hummingbird	Eastern United States and eastern Canada	10	House Wren	The United States (except southern areas) and southern Canada
5	Red-headed Woodpecker	Central and eastern United States and Canada	11	House Sparrow	Throughout the United States and Canada
6	Red-winged Blackbird	Throughout the United States and Canada	12	American Goldfinch	Throughout the United States and southern Canada

22

Name _____

All About Birds

Directions: Read about different birds. Then write about and draw a picture of your favorite one. Be ready to share this information with the class.

_____
(bird name)

Where does your bird live? _____

_____

What does your bird eat? _____

_____

What kind of nest does it build? _____

_____

Where does your bird usually nest? _____

_____

Some interesting facts about my bird: _____

_____

_____

Chicken Little

Retold by Steven Kellogg

Summary

Steven Kellogg does a marvelous job of retelling this timeless classic tale of chain reaction panic. Chicken Little and her friends, alarmed that the sky is falling, become easy prey to a hungry gourmet, Foxy Loxy, who disguises himself as a police officer. But his hopes of enjoying southern-fried chicken and spicy-sauced duck are dashed as he is brought to justice. Chicken Little lives to tell her grandchildren about her adventures on the day the acorn landed.

The outline below is a suggested plan for using the various activities that are presented in this unit. You may adapt these ideas to fit your own classroom situation.

Sample Plan

Lesson 1

- Continue Bird Watch Diary (page 17).
- Discuss cover of *Chicken Little*.
- Analyze parts of a Wanted Poster and chart adjectives (page 25).
- Read *Chicken Little*. Review the story (page 28).
- Create Wanted Posters (page 29).

Lesson 2

- Fill in the Story Frame (page 30).
- Send home Just In Case letters (page 31).
- Reread Kellogg's *Chicken Little*.
- Introduce Readers' Theater (pages 32-34).
- Compare different story versions (page 26) and do Comparing Stories (page 35).

Lesson 3

- Solve the Bird Message (page 53).
- Continue diary entries.
- Perform science experiments (page 55) and complete Scientific Method Report (page 56).

Lesson 4

- Sing Very Tweet Music (page 64).
- Match quotations in Whooo Said That? (page 36).
- Continue diary entries.

Lesson 5

- Practice Readers' Theater.
- Write a letter using A Word of Advice (page 37).
- Continue diary entries.

Lesson 6

- Do Bird Word Problems (page 52).
- Update "What We've Learned about Birds" (page 6).
- Measure eggs in "Eggs"actly the Right Size (page 38).
- Practice Readers' Theater.

Lesson 7

- Complete Bird Brainstorm (page 49).
- Label Bird Parts (page 58).
- Complete Bird Watch Diary and discuss.

Lesson 8

- Choose some of the art activities on pages 66-68.
- Make Pop-Up Invitations (pages 71-72).
- Culminating Activity: Readers' Theater Presentation (page 71).
- Distribute Awards (page 78).

Overview of Activities

SETTING THE STAGE

1. Some new additions to your learning center will encourage investigation. Rotate books you display. (Don't forget to include class books.) Add items such as a down pillow, pen and quill, empty egg cartons (items from birds that contribute to our life).

2. Continue checking progress in the incubator and taking bird walks with the class. Ask students to record data in their diaries and talk about student entries periodically. Keep these in student Bird Folders.

3. Investigate your community for people with farm poultry knowledge. Arrange a visit to a poultry farm or an aviary, if possible.

4. Sing "Old Mac Donald Had a Farm" using only birds that would be on a farm.

5. Survey class as to how many children have heard the story of Chicken Little? Henny Penny? Chicken Licken? Foxy Loxy?

ENJOYING THE BOOK

1. As you show students the cover of *Chicken Little*, have them predict the plot based on the title and illustrations. Discuss the term "retold."

2. Open to the Wanted Poster and read it to the children. Reread the adjectives. Ask students how they feel about Foxy Loxy. (What do you know about him from these words?) Explain that words such as rude, mean, and shrewd describe, or tell what kind of character Foxy Loxy is. Discuss the purpose and content of a wanted poster.

3. Read the book *Chicken Little* by Steven Kellogg. Be sure to share all pages slowly so the students get a chance to enjoy the humorous drawings. (This is a delightful book for the children to be able to enjoy individually.) Discuss the story with the class using suggestions from page 28.

4. Read Ruth Heller's book *Many Luscious Lollipops* (bibliography, page 79) to increase students' understanding of adjectives. Brainstorm adjectives that might describe other characters and objects from *Chicken Little*. List these on a display chart. If students have difficulty finding descriptive words, hand out bags of objects (ball, cotton, toy, for example) to small groups. Have each make a list of words that describe the objects (cotton—soft, white, fluffy).

   Have students design the wanted posters on page 29 using some of the adjectives on the list.

5. Complete the story frame for *Chicken Little* (page 30). Discuss the most important ideas necessary for the retelling of the story. You may first wish to model a story frame from a recently read book.

Overview of Activities *(cont.)*

ENJOYING THE BOOK (cont.)

6. Distribute the Just In Case letters (page 31). Explain the purpose of the assignment and ask students to discuss this page at home. Have students share responses in class the next day.

7. Review the use of quotation marks to show dialogue. Distribute copies of Whooo Said That? (page 36) and ask students to match characters with sentences and tell why they made their choices.

EXTENDING THE BOOK

1. Readers' Theater-*Chicken Licken* (pages 32-34) is presented as a culminating activity on pages 71-72. Read the play with the class. Assign parts and make plans and a schedule for practice times, designing scenery, etc. Prepare and send invitations (pages 71-72).

2. Read another version of *Chicken Little* (bibliography, page 79) or use Readers' Theater (pages 32-34) to compare the characters and plots. As a class, discuss the similarities and differences between the two stories. Ask which version students enjoyed the most and why. Complete the Comparing Stories Venn diagram (page 35) together or in small groups.

3. Answer the bulletin board questions (page 76). Complete the list of "Things We've Learned About Birds." Students can use information from activities kept in folders. They will be surprised at how much information they have gathered.

4. Solve Bird Word Problems (page 52) in cooperative groups using the facts provided. Put answers in boxes. Ask groups to explain how they arrived at their solutions.

5. Duplicate Solve the Bird Message (page 53). Have students use the code to solve the adage. Discuss student opinions about which came first. Challenge them to find the meanings of the four adages.

6. Ornithologists Want To Know (page 55) provides simple experiments that students can perform in small groups. Provide materials from page 55 and copies of page 56 for each group. (You may choose to do some or all of the activities.) When experiments are completed, have groups fill in the Scientific Method Report. Discuss the importance of using the scientific method as a systematic means of collecting and recording data.

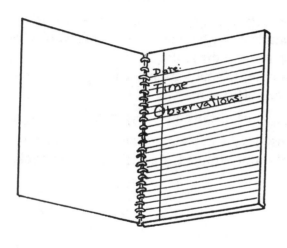 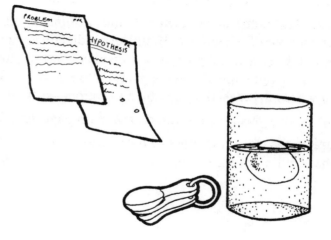 

Overview of Activities *(cont.)*

EXTENDING THE BOOK *(cont.)*

7. Chicken Little created havoc with her claim that the sky was falling. Ask students what they would do in a situation where a friend acted in a ridiculous manner. Brainstorm ways of dealing with the circumstances. Distribute A Word of Advice (page 37) and have students write a letter of advice to a friend.

8. Investigate and compare the sizes of bird eggs using "Eggs"actly The Right Size activity (page 38). *Bird* by David Burnie, contains several outstanding pages of photographs on egg shapes, sizes, and colors.

9. Expand student word banks while using parts of speech to develop new lyrics for "Farmer-in-the-Dell" (page 43). Sing familiar tunes in which birds are mentioned. Add movement where possible. Very Tweet Music (page 64) has more suggestions.

10. Provide cooperative group experience while reviewing students' knowledge of birds by completing Bird Brainstorm (page 49). Students can use accumulated material from folders as well as Learning Center and other classroom resources.

11. Have students match the description clues in Who's Who (page 62) to the bird pictures. Discuss each bird adding facts from other sources, if possible. Keep these in bird folders.

12. Choose one or more of the art activities on pages 66-68 to decorate the classroom, or attach to student poetry, reports, and books.

13. Use Cracked Egg Sentences (page 48) to review sentence structure and punctuation. Students can create their own by making an egg sentence puzzle. Combine student eggs into a class Cracked Egg Sentence Book (with answer key) for students to enjoy.

14. Build upon students' word banks with Bird Detective (page 47). Challenge students to design their own word search using other bird categories.

Reviewing the Story

The following questions and activities can be used to recapture the events in the story and encourage students to take a closer look at the characters.

Questions for Discussion:

1. What plans did Foxy Loxy have for Chicken Little and her friends? How does the author help you to "see" this better?

2. Can the sky fall? Why do you suppose Chicken Little's friends believed her?

3. How did Chicken Little's panic get everyone into trouble? Discuss actual situations where panic can be dangerous.

4. Foxy Loxy was sly. How did he trick Chicken Little and her friends?

5. Explain how Chicken Little discovered that the policeman was Foxy Loxy.

6. The little acorn played a big part in creating a happy ending for Chicken Little. Ask students to retell the events from the point where Foxy Loxy threw the acorn.

Related Activities:

1. Review rhyming name patterns such as Foxy Loxy, Goosey Lucy, Ducky Lucky, Turkey Lurkey and Henny Penny. Ask students to name others and make up similar word patterns.

2. Recall the sequence of events by making a "Who Came Along Next?" chart (see below). Label sentence strips with the character's names. (A pocket chart is helpful here.) Ask students to arrange them in order of appearance. Capsulize what happened when each character was introduced. Discuss Foxy Loxy's reactions to each new character as he checked his recipe book (see pictures in book). For example, when Ducky Lucky came along Foxy Loxy "shivered with greed."

Character Chart
Who Came Along Next?

Foxy Loxy	Turkey Lurkey
Chicken Little	Goosey Loosey
Ducky Lucky	Henny Penny

3. Discuss the meaning of the following words /sayings: feather-weight; light as a feather; sly as a fox; hen-pecked; "your goose is cooked"; "you're chicken."

4. The beautifully detailed illustrations in the story convey thoughts, actions, and feelings. Show some of the pages again and discuss how the pictures enhance the context of the story.

5. Ask students to draw pictures of their favorite scenes in the story and write captions for them. Design a title, "The Sky is Falling," above the pictures and cut pieces of blue paper, white clouds and flying birds to create the illusion of a falling sky.

Name _____

Wanted Poster

Directions: In the story of Chicken Little, Foxy Loxy appeared on a wanted poster. Make your own wanted poster. Try to use as many describing words as you can. Draw a picture.

Name_____

Story Frame

The story takes place _____

_____

The main character's name is _____

A problem occurs when _____

_____

_____

After that _____

_____

and _____

_____

The problem is solved when _____

_____

_____

The story ends with _____

_____

_____

_____

Name _____

Just In Case

Dear Parents,

After reading the book *Chicken Little*, we decided that it would be wise to review our emergency information. Please help us by making sure that your child knows the following procedures:

1. How and when to dial 911. (Role play with your child "Would this be an emergency?" You fell and skinned your knee. You see smoke coming from a neighbor's house, etc.)

2. How to say his/her name, address, and phone number clearly.

3. The name of a grown up friend or neighbor who could help in an emergency.

4. What to do about strangers.

5. The name of your family doctor.

- -

Thank you for helping us remember our emergency information.

Please sign and return this portion to class by_____.

We have reviewed safety information at our house.

_____
Child's name

_____
Parent's signature

Readers' Theater—*Chicken Licken*

Cast: Narrator; Foxy Woxy; Chicken Licken; Ducky Lucky; Cocky Locky; Goosey Loosey; Turkey Lurkey: Henny Penny

Note: The book version should have been read to the children several times. Students should have an opportunity to act out the story and retell it in various ways. Readers' Theater is not a memorized script but one with which students are very familiar. Remind the students to stand with good posture. Emphasize proper voice projection and clarity when speaking. Have students place the strips in folders when performing.

Narrator: Welcome to our Readers' Theater presentation of Chicken Licken. There are many versions of this favorite old story; this is ours. Our characters are Chicken Licken . . .

Chicken: Peep, peep, peep!

Narrator: Henny Penny . . .

Henny: Cluck, cluck, cluck

Narrator: Cocky Locky . . .

Cocky: Cock-a-doodle-doo!

Narrator: Ducky Lucky . . .

Ducky: Quack, quack, quack!

Narrator: Goosey Loosey . . .

Goosey: Honk, honk, honk!

Narrator: Turkey Lurkey . . .

Turkey: Gobble, gobble, gobble!

Narrator: And Foxy Woxy.

Foxy: (smiles and licks lips)

All animals: (Make animals sounds as Foxy Woxy licks lips!)

Narrator: One day, Chicken Licken was scratching for corn in the barnyard when— plop—an acorn hit (him/her) on the head.

Chicken: Oh, good gracious me! The sky is falling! I must go and tell the King!

Narrator: So (he/she) went along and went along until (he/she) met Henny Penny.

Henny: Good morning, Chicken Licken, where are you going?

Chicken: Oh, Henny Penny, the sky is falling and I am going to tell the King.

Henny: How do you know the sky is falling?

32

Readers' Theater *(cont.)*

Chicken:	I saw it with my own eyes, I heard it with my own ears, and a piece of it fell on my own head.
Henny:	Then I will go with you.
Narrator:	So they went along and they went along until they met Cocky Locky.
Cocky:	Good morning, Henny Penny and Chicken Licken, where are you going?
Henny:	Oh Cocky Locky, the sky is falling and we are going to tell the King.
Cocky:	How do you know the sky is falling?
Henny:	Chicken Licken told me.
Chicken:	I saw it with my own eyes, I heard it with my own ears, and a piece of it fell on my own head.
Cocky:	Then I will go with you and we will tell the king.
Narrator:	So they went along and they went along until they met Ducky Lucky.
Ducky:	Good morning Cocky Locky, Henny Penny, and Chicken Licken. Where are you going?
Cocky:	Oh, Ducky Lucky, the sky is falling and we are going to tell the King.
Ducky:	How do you know the sky is falling?
Cocky:	Henny Penny told me.
Henny:	Chicken Licken told me.
Chicken:	I saw it with my own eyes, I heard it with my own ears, and a piece of it fell on my own head.
Ducky:	Then I will go with you and we will tell the King.
Narrator:	So they went along and they went along until they met Goosey Loosey.
Goosey:	Good morning Ducky Lucky, Cocky Locky, Henny Penny, and Chicken Licken. Where are you going?
Ducky:	Oh, Goosey Loosey, the sky is falling and we are going to tell the King.
Goosey:	How do you know the sky is falling?
Ducky:	Cocky Locky told me.
Cocky:	Henny Penny told me.
Henny:	Chicken Licken told me.
Narrator:	(to audience) Everybody together - repeat 'I saw it with my own eyes, I heard it with my own ears, and a piece of it fell on my own head.'
Goosey:	Then I will go with you and we will tell the King.
Narrator:	So they went along and they went along until they met Turkey Lurkey.
Turkey:	Good morning Goosey Loosey, Ducky Lucky, Cocky Locky, Henny Penny, and Chicken Licken, where are you all going?

Readers' Theater *(cont.)*

Goosey: Oh, Turkey Lurkey, the sky is falling and we are going to tell the King.

Turkey: How do you know the sky is falling?

Goosey: Ducky Lucky told me.

Ducky: Cocky Locky told me.

Cocky: Henny Penny told me.

Henny: Chicken Licken told me.

Narrator: (to audience) Everybody together - repeat 'I saw it with my own eyes, I heard it with my own ears, and a piece of it fell on my own head.'

Turkey: Then I will go with you and we will tell the King.

Narrator: So they went along and they went along until they met Foxy Woxy.

Foxy: Good morning, Turkey Lurkey, Goosey Loosey, Ducky Lucky, Cocky Locky, Henny Penny and Chicken Licken. Where are you all going?

Turkey: Oh, Foxy Woxy, the sky is falling and we are going to tell the King.

Foxy: But this is not the way to the King. Come with me I will show you a short cut to the King's palace.

Narrator: The short cut was really a path to Foxy Woxy's den. Chicken Licken was the first to figure out what Foxy Woxy was up to. But, strangely enough, he didn't panic. He looked around and noticed something over by the huge oak tree.

Chicken: Foxy Woxy, I heard a cry of help over by that old tree. It sounds like my cousin, Rooster Booster.

Narrator: Foxy Woxy, being the sly and hungry fellow he was, dashed over to the tree. But when he got there, a huge trapper's net came crashing down upon his head.

Foxy: Help me, Chicken Licken! Help me, Henny Penny! Someone help me!

Chicken: Oh, my! What happened? Did the sky fall, Foxy?

Narrator: With that, everyone began to laugh, and laugh, and laugh.
Goosey Loosey waddled over to the King's palace and told him what had happened. His soldiers carried Foxy Woxy far, far away. He has not been heard from since!

Name

Comparing Stories

Decide how the two Chicken Little stories are alike and how they are different. Fill in the pictures below after discussing each story.

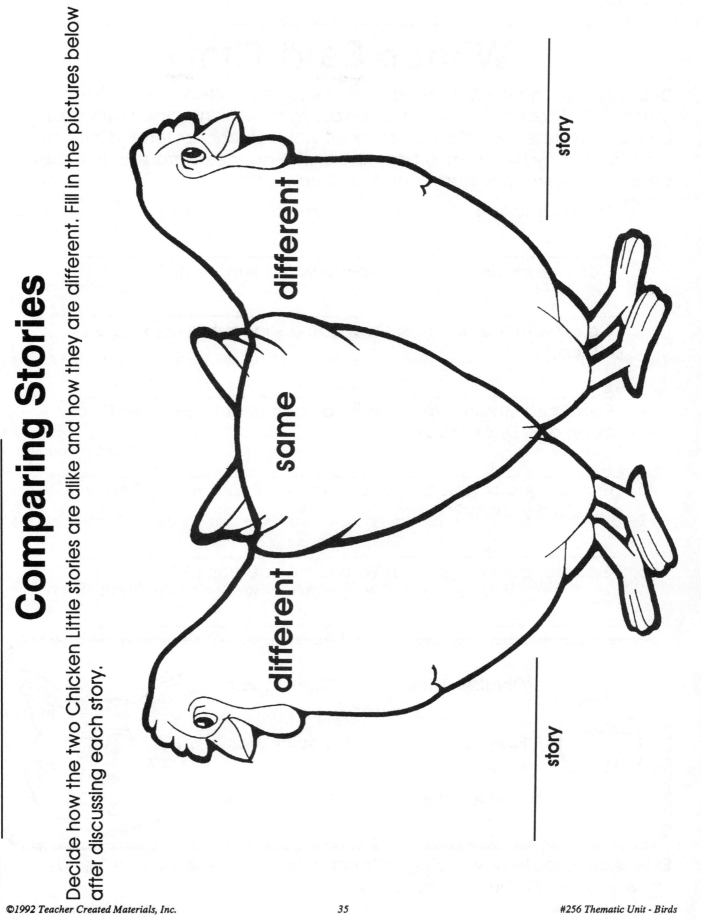

story

different

same

different

story

Name _____

Whooo Said That?

Directions: To show what characters are saying, writers use quotation marks (" "). These marks help the reader to tell which words were spoken by the character. Here are six sentences which characters in *Chicken Little* or *Henny Penny* may have spoken. Find the characters in the box below and write their names on the correct lines.

1. "The sky is falling. A piece of it hit me on the head."

   _____

2. "Cock-a-doodle-doo! Where are you going, Henny Penny?"

   _____

3. "Come with me and I will show you a shortcut to the King's palace."

   _____

4. "Honk, honk, honk! Where are you going, Henny Penny, Cocky Locky, and Ducky Lucky?"

   _____

5. "Quack, quack, quack! Where are you going Henny Penny and Cocky Locky?"

   _____

6. "Gobble, gobble, gobble! Where are you going?"

   _____

 **Chicken Little**   **Ducky Lucky**

Foxy Loxy   **Cocky Locky**

Goosey Lucy   **Turkey Lurkey**

Extension: Create new dialogue for characters and see if your friends know who would be likely to say it.

Name _____

A Word of Advice

Chicken Little is your friend. You find her crying about the sky falling on her head. This isn't the first time your friend has said something so ridiculous. As her friend you want to talk to her about this, so you decide to write her a letter. What advice would you give to Chicken Little?

Dear Chicken Little,

_____

_____

_____

_____

_____

_____

_____

Your friend,

_____

Name _____

"Eggs"actly the Right Size

Directions: Cut out the ruler below to measure the length of each egg. Write the length in the blank next to each egg.

Duck egg

Hummingbird egg

_____

_____

Chicken egg

_____

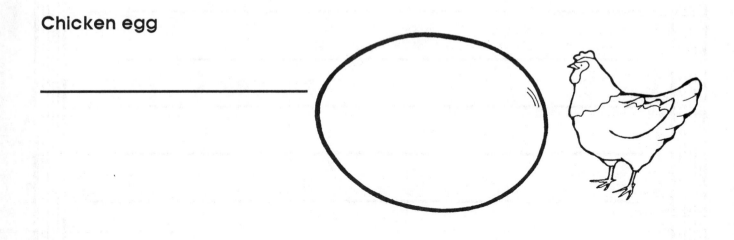

The _____ egg was the longest.

The _____ egg was the shortest.

Inches	1		2		3		4		5		6	
Centimeters	1	2	3	4	5	6	7	8	9	10	11	12	13	14	15	16	17

Extension: Compare extra large, medium and small eggs from the market.

Writing Activities

Using the Bird Folder

It's a good idea to have students keep and compile a booklet of information daily as they read books about a subject or theme. Their pages can be used as a study or reference guide for when they do a culminating story or write a paper based on the theme. After constructing Bird Folders (page 6), encourage students to use them frequently as a resource and to store important documents and activities from the unit in them.

Bird Watch Diary/Incubator Observations

Before you begin your class bird watching be sure the class has read *Feathers for Lunch*. Discuss the question "What made the birds fly?" Talk about "quietly observing" for whatever time limit your class can handle. You may want to make binoculars (page 16) to encourage looking. It may enhance your bird watching to read Buffet for Birds (page 57). Discuss sitting quietly, sketching, and writing. You may want to make an overhead transparency of page 17 to model what you expect from your students. Remember to observe at the same time daily.

For class observations of the incubator you may want to set up a schedule of names and times, allowing all to see without crowding.

Author's Chair

Designate a chair in your classroom to be "The Author's Chair."   (You may want to decorate a pillow case and slip it over the back of the chair for a special touch.) Whenever students have published works of their own to read they sit in the chair and others listen.

Bird Facts

Bird Name	Colors and Markings	Where It Lives	Interesting Facts

Each student will need a Bird Facts worksheet (page 40) for writing information gained daily during the bird unit. The information may be gathered from whole group reading and sharing by the teacher or students, the individual's reading, or others reading at the Author's Chair. Facts can be gathered during one of the science experiments or on a bird walk. This writing can be done as a whole class lesson, in cooperative groups, or individually. (Note: Try different ways to record information on different days.)

Name _____

Bird Facts

Bird Name	Colors and Markings	Where It Lives	Interesting Facts

Creating a Cinquain

A cinquain is a five line poem. A word cinquain is made up of the following lines:

> **Line 1** - One word which *names* the subject.
>
> **Line 2** - Two words which *define or describe* the subject.
>
> **Line 3** - Three words which *express action* associated with the subject.
>
> **Line 4** - A *four word phrase* about the subject.
>
> **Line 5** - One word which *sums up, restates, or supplies a synonym* for the subject.

Here is a good opportunity to introduce describing words and/or review nouns, verbs and synonyms. The following activities will provide students with word lists which can be used for bird cinquains.

1. Read the cinquain "Chicken." Display it on a pocket chart or chalkboard and discuss cinquains.

    Chicken
    Plump, Brown
    Scratching, Pecking, Clucking
    Sitting on her eggs
    Hen

2. List all of the bird names mentioned in *Feathers for Lunch* on a 12" x 18" (30 cm x 45 cm) piece of construction paper. These will become the subject choices for cinquains.

3. Talk about the describing words called adjectives. Use a second piece of construction paper (a different color) and brainstorm as many adjectives for birds as possible. It may be helpful for students to describe the bird by saying "It is a _____ bird."

4. Discuss line three in the cinquain "Chicken," noting that these express action. This time use a third color of paper and brainstorm verbs for birds.

5. Ask students to name a four word phrase describing a bird. Break into small groups and discuss the students' responses. Use a fourth paper color to list the phrases submitted.

6. Finally, make a student generated list of synonyms for birds on yet another color of construction paper.

Subjects	Describing words	Action words
Wren Cardinal woodpecker	Soft beautiful graceful	Soaring flying Singing

Phrases	Synonyms
builds a Strong nest. lives in the forest	bird aviator

Hang all five lists in the order in which they will be used for the cinquain. (Point out that "cinq" means five in French, thus explaining the derivation of the term cinquain.)

Put numbers above each list to indicate how many choices are to be made from each category. Provide students with page 42 and allow them to create their own cinquains. Students can read their poems to the class and/or display them. These can be mounted on a large tree made of construction or butcher paper and surrounded by birds.

Name_____

My Cinquain Poem

_____
noun
(the subject)

_____ , _____
adjective   **adjective**
(describing word)   (describing word)

_____ , _____ , _____
verb   **verb**   **verb**
(action word)   (action word)   (action word)

_____
4 word phrase
(about the subject)

_____
synonym
(another word for subject)

"Farmer-in-the-Dell" Chant

Create delightful and amusing new songs by combining word banks with the tune to "Farmer-in-the-Dell." Emphasize the poetic verse within the lyrics.

- Brainstorm the following categories with your class. (Words provided here may be used in addition to those generated by students or to help them get started.)

Adjectives *describing words*	Nouns *who*	Verbs *action*	Prepositional Phrases *where they go*
big	birds	fly	to the south
huge	sparrows	soar	in the barnyard
enormous	chickens	glide	over the mountain tops
tiny	ducks	migrate	across the lake
miniature	owls	flutter	to the shore
fat	gulls	paddle	in the grass
skinny	penguins	swim	high in the sky
giant	peacocks	roost	into the water
pretty	pelicans	preen	along the shore
beautiful	ducks	waddle	through the park
fluffy	parakeets	molt	on the ice

- Review each category immediately after brainstorming. Then go to the next list.
- Choose two adjectives, and one noun, and sing the first line of "Farmer-in-the-Dell" : *"Big, huge, birds, big, huge, birds"*
- Next add a verb and phrase: *"Big, huge birds fly to the south"*
- End with the first line: *"Big, huge, birds"*

The Amazing Owl Report

*See suggested activity 10, page 9.

Bird Word Bank

Cut pieces of butcher paper into shapes similar to those below, or use simple geometric shapes. Fill them in with the words compiled by the students from this unit and supplement it with the words provided on this page. Post word banks around the classroom for students to use in daily written and oral language experiences.

Words can be reinforced in a variety of ways:

- Write words on an index card and have students put them in alphabetical order; make sentences with each word; tell what each word means.
- Draw a picture to illustrate each word.
- Write a story with some of the words and share it with the class.
- Make word scrambles, word searches, and puzzles.

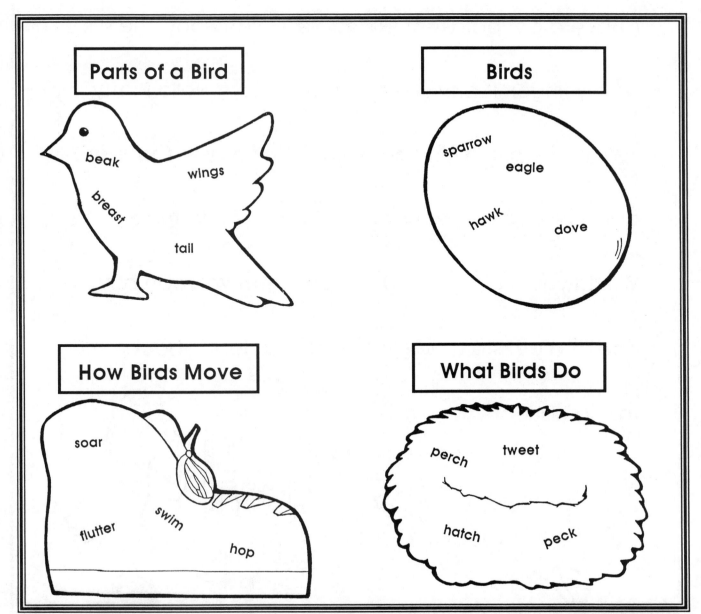

Parts of a Bird

beak
wings
breast
tail

Birds

sparrow
eagle
hawk
dove

How Birds Move

soar
flutter
swim
hop

What Birds Do

perch
tweet
hatch
peck

Name _____

Punctuation Peck

Directions: Read the following paragraph. Add the correct punctuation to make the paragraph easier to understand. If capitals are needed, put the capital letter above the incorrect letter. Hint: There are 23 mistakes.

My Pet Bird

i have a pet parakeet His name is pretty boy. he sits

on my finger Pretty Boy can talk he says, Hello Pretty

Boy im teaching him more tricks His favorite foods are:

apples sunflower seeds potato chips and lettuce.

Would you like to have a pet parakeet you can buy

one at a pet store be sure to read a book about

taking care of your bird

46

Name _____

Bird Detective

Follow the directions below to make your own word search.

1. Copy eight words from the Bird Word Bank onto the lines below.
2. Place each word in the graph squares. Remember, you can write a word vertically, horizontally, or diagonally.
3. Fill in the rest of the squares with letters.
4. Exchange your word search with a partner. Be a detective and try to find all of the words listed on your partner's word search.

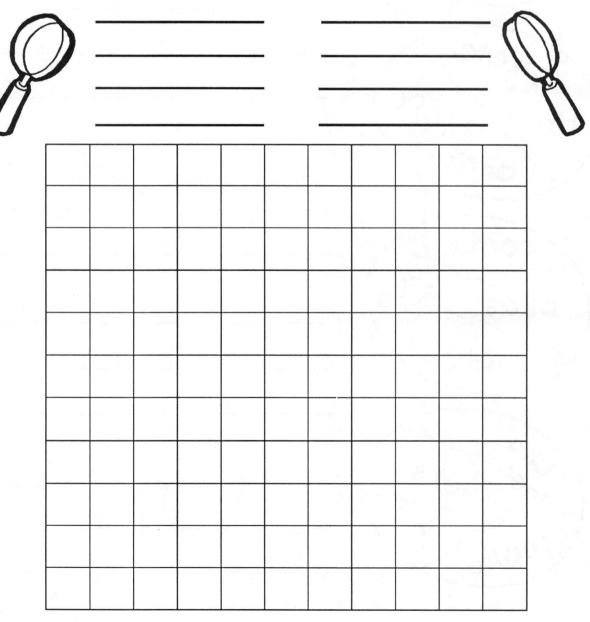

Cracked Egg Sentences

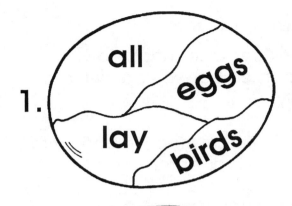

1.

all eggs lay birds

Directions: The words in each egg can be put together to make a sentence. Write each sentence on the line next to its egg. Be sure to use the correct sentence punctuation.

1. _____

_____

_____

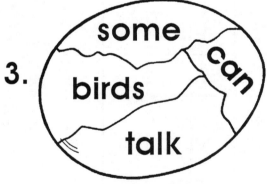

2.

watch you do birds

2. _____

_____

_____

3.

some birds can talk

3. _____

_____

_____

4.

bird feeder let's make a

4. _____

_____

Bird Brainstorm

Directions: Brainstorm with your group to decide on some endings to the following phrases. Share your group answers with the whole class or exchange ideas with classmates at the author's chair.

1. The egg began to crack when _____

   _____

   _____

2. The owl flew from its branch to _____

   _____

   _____

3. To build its nest, the house sparrow found _____

   _____

   _____

4. While flying, the eagle spotted _____

   _____

   _____

5. The hen stopped scratching _____

   _____

   _____

6. During migration the swallow _____

   _____

   _____

7. The hummingbird was attracted by _____

   _____

   _____

8. The turkey was nervous because _____

   _____

   _____

Class Big Book

To make class Big Books, divide the class into small, cooperative groups. Pass out pocket chart strips (page 14) to each group and let them decide what comes out of the egg. These can be glued to Big Book pages and illustrated. As an alternative, groups can choose a specific bird and write bird facts and make illustrations on the page.

Story titles such as "The Adventures of Chirpy," or fictional story starter ideas could be used to spark creative writing stories for class Big Books as well. Illustrate the text with drawings, finger painting, collages, etc. Don't forget a cover page, a table of contents, and a back page.

Display the book pages on your classroom wall for all to see, or bind it to make a book. Loan your book to your school library, other classrooms, or even your local public library. Students also enjoy checking out class-created Big Books overnight to share at home.

Put the Hen in the Henhouse

Directions: Two to four children can play. Each player takes a turn connecting two adjacent dots with a line going across or down. If a line completes a square, the player initials the box and takes another turn. The game continues until all dots have been connected. Score 1 point for each empty, completed box, 3 points for each box that catches an egg, and 5 points for each hen box. The player with the most points wins.

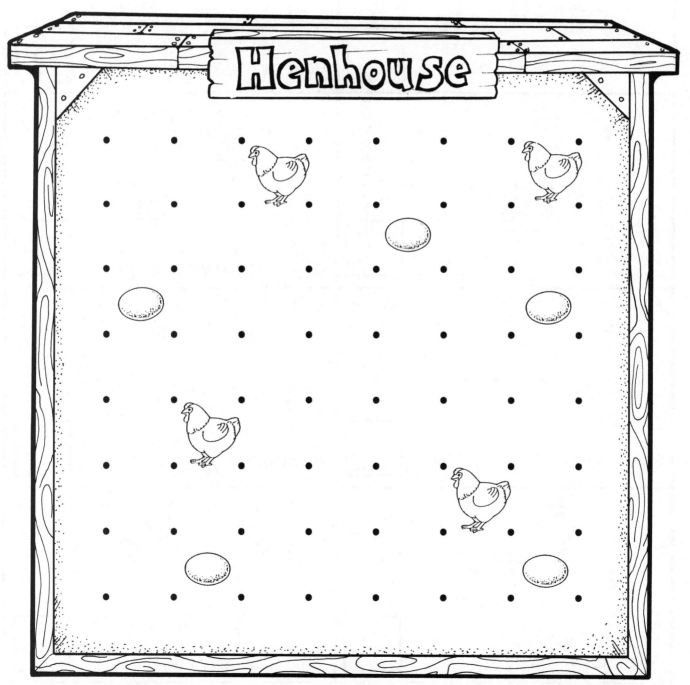

Bird Word Problems

*See activity 4, page 26 for directions.

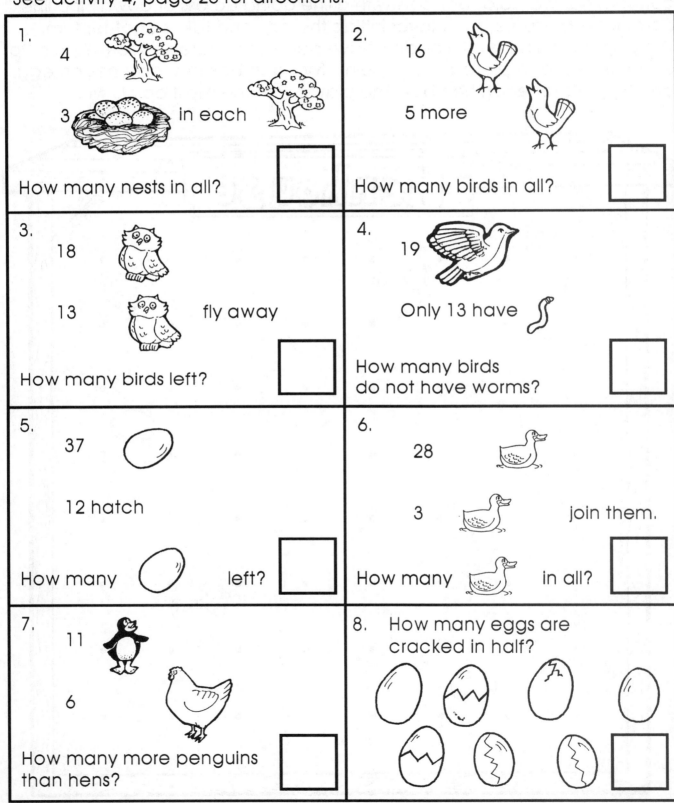

1.
4

3   in each

How many nests in all?

2.
16

5 more

How many birds in all?

3.
18

13   fly away

How many birds left?

4.
19

Only 13 have

How many birds
do not have worms?

5.
37

12 hatch

How many   left?

6.
28

3   join them.

How many   in all?

7.
11

6

How many more penguins
than hens?

8.   How many eggs are
     cracked in half?

Name _____

Solve the Bird Message

Below is a famous saying about birds. Solve the problems in each box below. Then find the answer under the word blank and place the letter from the box on the matcing blank.

___ ___ ___ ___ ___   ___ ___ ___ ___   ___ ___ ___ ___ ___ , ___ ___ ___
32 13 43 38 13   38 35 87 29   21 43 10 48 33   33 13 29

___ ___ ___ ___ ___ ___ ___   ___ ___   ___ ___ ___   ___ ___ ___ ?
38 13 43 38 65 29 64   1 10   33 13 29   29 59 59

O 16 − 15	H 26 − 13	T 30 + 3	W 42 − 10	E 22 + 7
I 67 − 24	F 38 − 17	G 48 +11	A 22 +13	C 15 + 23
M 63 + 24	R 42 − 32	N 68 − 4	S 23 + 25	K 89 − 24

I think the _____ came first because _____

_____

Here are 4 other sayings you may have heard:

"A bird in the hand is worth 2 in the bush."

"The early bird catches the worm."

"Don't put all of your eggs in one basket."

"Don't count your chickens before they hatch."

Try to find out what these mean. Ask friends, family, and teachers, or use library books. Report back to class on what you learned.

Attributes of Birds

- Birds have feathers.

- They lay eggs with hard shells.

- They have two legs.

- They have two wings. Most birds can fly.

- Birds have a beak.

- Most birds can see much better than other animals, including people.

- Most birds have a good sense of hearing.

- Birds are vertebrates (animals with backbones).

54

Ornithologists Want to Know

Will an egg float?

Materials: 2 glasses of plain water; 1 teaspoon; 1 raw egg; salt

Procedure: Try floating the egg in each glass of water. What happens? Now add 1 teaspoon of salt to one glass and stir. Add more salt. Repeat until egg floats. Tally how many teaspoons of salt it took to float the egg.

Is the egg raw or boiled?

Materials: 1 boiled egg; 1 raw egg

Procedure: Take turns spinning the eggs on a table top. (One will spin easily; one will spin with wobbles.) Label each. Crack each open to see which chicken egg is raw and which is boiled.

Can I see through an egg shell?

Materials: a raw egg; vinegar; bowl

Procedure: Soak a raw egg in vinegar to take the calcium out of the eggshell. It will feel like rubber and you can see through to the inside. (The vinegar should cover the egg in a glass container overnight.)

Is a bird bone really hollow?

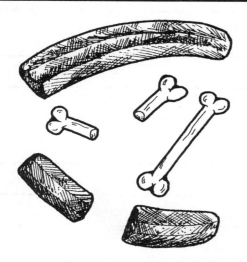

Materials: clean, dry chicken and beef bones; hammer and/or saw

Procedure: Hold both kinds of bones up to the light. Are there any differences? Use the hammer or saw to open a chicken bone. Discuss what you see. Now use the hammer or saw on the beef bone and discuss what happens.

Note: This activity must be done by the teacher. However, students should have the opportunity to handle and compare the bones at a display table or in the Learning Center.

Scientific Method Report

A little birdie told me you'd want to know...

We did a science experiment.

It was about _____

_____

Our question was _____

_____

Our hypothesis (guess) was _____

_____

_____

Our experiment (what we did) was _____

_____

_____

The result (what happened) was_____

_____

_____

Our conclusion (why it happened) was _____

_____

_____

_____

Buffet for Birds

Setting up a feeding station is a great way to attract and watch birds. Here are a few ideas for how to make some simple feeders using inexpensive materials you can find around the house.

Bird Food Garlands
String popcorn, fruit bits, and bread on loops of thread. Hang them on tree branches.

Pie Tin Feeder
Hammer an old pie tin to the top of an old broom handle or wooden dowel. Press the dowel into the ground. Scatter seeds in the pie tin.

Pine Cone Feeder
Roll a pine cone in thin sugary icing and then in seeds. Or, stuff bits of bread and fruit into a pine cone and hang the feeder by tying the string to a branch.

Plastic Net Bags
The same net bags that onions, garlic, and potatoes come packaged in can become bird feeders. Simply fill them with bread, fruits, and seeds and hang them in trees.

Plastic Container Feeder
Cut a hole several inches in diameter in the side of a well-cleaned bleach or milk container. Tie a string through the handle and hang it from a tree. Fill the bottom of container with bird seed.

Suggestions: You may want to divide into small groups to plan a feeding experiment using homemade feeders and different types of bird food. Teams will need to investigate birds in your area, types of food different birds prefer, and shelters birds like. Remember, birds are affected by food, water and shelter.

Note: Additional bird feeder suggestions can be found in *Our Environment* Thematic Unit #272 (Teacher Created Materials, Inc., 1991).

Bird Parts

Directions: Parts of the picture below are labeled. But the letters are mixed up. Find out what the labels say by using the words in the Word Bank. On each line write the correct word above the scrambled one. Then color the picture.

Word Bank

bill	breast
eye	tail
foot	crown
wing	neck
leg	

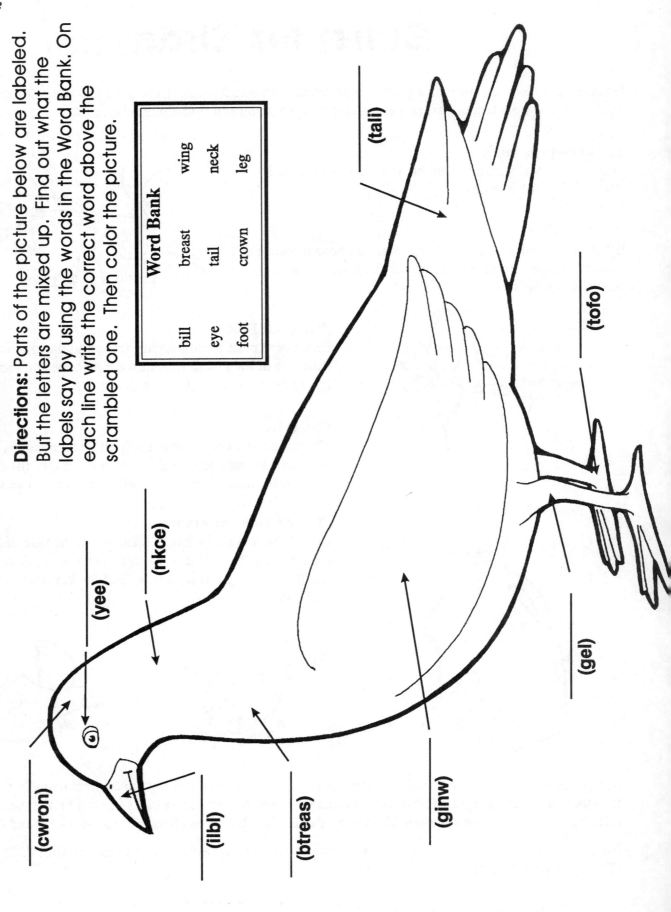

(tali)

(tofo)

(nkce)

(yee)

(gel)

(cwron)

(ilbl)

(btreas)

(ginw)

Name

58

Making a Chick Incubator

Hatching chicks will be a highlight of your year and you will probably want to repeat it annually once you see how easily it can be accomplished. However, before you begin make sure you have homes for the hatched chicks. Also schedule the incubator for 21 days of uninterrupted school so you won't miss the big event during a vacation.

Materials: rectangular foam ice chest; transparent plastic; library tape; light socket and cord; light bulb; small dish for water; thermostat (available at pet supply or feed stores); skills knife; newspaper; fertilized eggs

Directions:

1. Cut two viewing windows (about 4 inches/10 cm in diameter) in the ice chest (one in the top and one in an end). Cover them with transparent plastic held in place by library tape. Cut a small hole in the center of the end opposite the end viewing window. It should be about halfway from the top to the bottom of the chest and just large enough for the empty socket to fit through. Below the socket opening, make a small hole to insert wiring for the thermostat. (Follow manufacturer's directions for installation.)

2. Put the socket in the hole. Install the light bulb.

3. Install the thermostat and wiring as shown in the illustration above. Make sure the incubator remains at a constant 101 to 103 degrees Fahrenheit (38 to 39 degress Celsiuis) before placing eggs into the incubator.

4. Place newspaper on the floor of the incubator. Add a small dish of water to keep the air moist. Check and fill periodically.

5. Place eggs into incubator, turn three times a day from the 2nd to the 18th day, and wait patiently for 21 days.

   Encourage students to observe conditions within the incubator periodically and to record data in their diaries (page 8).

Building a Nest

The pictures below show birds building a nest. They are not in the correct order. Color each picture. Then cut out the boxes and put them in the correct order. Number in the circles from 1-6 to show the nest building steps. Glue the pictures on another piece of paper or staple them together for a picture book.

Mighty Eagle

Background Information

Eagles are one of the largest, most powerful birds in the world. When viewed up close, they appear fierce. While soaring above in search of food, they are incredibly graceful. Such traits have made the eagle a symbol of power and freedom. Roman warriors considered the figure of an eagle to be a sign of bravery and great strength. North American Indian warriors wore eagle feathers as a sign of bravery. In 1782, after some debate in Congress, the United States chose the bald eagle as its national bird.

Eagles generally live 20-30 years (50 years or more in captivity). The population has dropped due to pollution from industrial wastes and pesticides. They build their nests, called eyries, in tall trees, on cliff ledges, or among boulders, preferring a high lookout point to spot prey.

The bald eagle lives near lakes, large rivers, and the sea coast. Its diet consists mainly of fish. Bald eagles are diurnal, which means they fly and hunt for food during the day.

Activities

Discuss with students the places where they have seen our national bird. Choose one or more of these activities as a follow-up to the discussion.

- Clean a quarter (or any coin money) with a dampened paper towel and baking soda. Put paper on top of the quarter and rub with a crayon.
- Find out about other eagles, such as the golden eagle, the harpy eagle, and the monkey-eating eagle.
- Draw a picture of where a bald eagle might live.
- Draw a picture of an Indian headdress or design one with paper and paint.

Name _____

Who's Who?

Match the birds to the description. Cut the pictures at the bottom of the page along the dotted lines. Glue each bird's picture next to its description.

1. An owl is thought to be wise. It hunts at night.	2. The cardinal is the only red bird with a crest.	3. The hummingbird collects nectar with its long bill.

4. Woodpeckers peck holes in trees to gather insects.	5. Eagles' long, broad wings help them fly high.	6. A duck is a bird with webbed feet.

Fun and Games

Birdwalk Relays

Object of the Game: To have every team member do the announced bird imitation before competing teams.

Directions: Divide your class into teams. Designate a start and finish line. Explain that you will call out a bird name and demonstrate the action to be copied. Team members will relay back and forth until all members have had a turn. Students will go to the back of the line and sit after their turn. The team seated first earns 1 point. The team accumulating the most points wins.

Pigeon Walk—Students make wings by folding their hands up under their arms. (Turn feet in "pigeon toes" and touch knees together.)

Hummingbird Flutter—Bend arms up to flutter hands parallel to shoulders, bend knees, up on tip toes.

Penguin Stroll—Upright posture, arms at side with hands pointed to the back, feet pointed out, heels meeting. Have students waddle from side to side as they move.

Rooster Strut—Make wings, bend at the waist, bend knees, bob head.

Ostrich Step—Have students place arms at side with hands at hip level fluttering. Take giant steps with head bobbing.

Hint: Have children discuss birds they've learned about and their characteristics. Add these to the relays. Use "walks" to transition children, change groups, or line up.

Red Robin

This game is played in the same way as Red Rover.

Directions: Divide the class up into four or five groups, giving each group a bird name. Choose a student to start the game. Mark off two boundary lines about 50 feet (15m) apart. The caller (student chosen) stands midway between the boundaries and says "Red Robin, Red Robin, only_____come hopping," announcing which bird group may hop forward. As they approach the caller, he/she hops to tag students, who, if tagged, must then join the caller as taggers. The caller continues, changing bird names each time. The game is over when only one student is left untagged.

Vary the game to include other movements such as waddling, or hopping on one foot, or backwards.

Very Tweet Music

The following songs are familiar to many students. They can be found in *Tom Glazer's Treasury of Songs for Children* (bibliography, page 79). Ask students to bring in appropriate records and tapes to share.

"The Mulberry Bush"

This classic can be changed to reflect what your students have learned in a fun way that includes movement.

> *This is the way the eagle soars.*
> *The eagle soars* (2 times)
> *This is the way the eagle soars*
> *above the highest mountains.*

Add other verses which begin:

> *This is the way the rooster crows.*
> *This is the way the hummingbird hovers.*

"The Little White Duck"

> *There's a little white duck sitting in the water,*
> *A little white duck doing what he ought -er;*
> *He took a bite of a lily pad,*
> *Flapped his wings and he said, "I'm glad I'm a little white duck sitting in the water."*
> *Quack, quack, quack.*

"Go Tell Aunt Rhody"

---

1. *Go Tell Aunt Rhody,* (3 times)
   the old gray goose is dead.

2. *The one we've been saving,* (3 times)
   To make a feather bed.

3. *She died on Friday,* (3 times)
   With an aching in her head.

4. *Old gander's weeping,* (3 times)
   Because his wife is dead.

5. *Goslings are mourning,* (3 times)
   Because their mother's dead.

6. *Go tell Aunt Rhody,* (3 times)
   The old gray goose is dead.

Other tunes you may wish to include in your repertoire are: "Rockin' Robin"; "Feed the Birds"; "Turkey in the Straw."

64

Name _____

Create an Egghead

Directions: Design as many interesting faces as you can in the egg shapes below. Try to draw each one a little different from the others. Can you make a face that is happy, sad, surprised, angry, or confused? When you finish, share your faces with a friend.

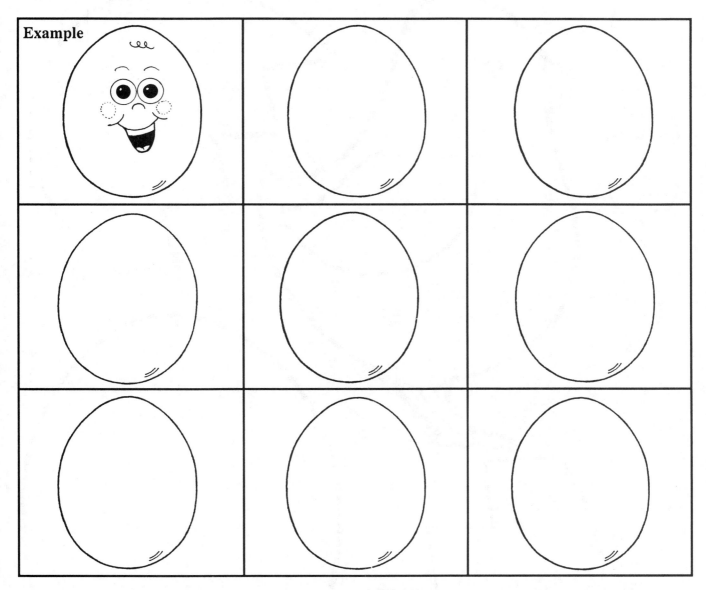

An "Eggs"tra Idea:

Bring in a plastic pop-apart egg. Make a character that you would like to see hatch from it. It could be real or imaginary. Or, glue the egg shut and decorate it as an egghead character.

Egg Mobile

Directions: Make copies of the pattern below on construction paper or trace on stiff poster board for students to use as patterns. Attach pieces with yarn and suspend the mobiles from the ceiling or a wire line to decorate your room.

66

Name _____

Springtime in the Country

Directions: Turn winter to spring with your crayons.

Make green grass grow.

Draw a bird's nest and birds.

Draw flowers.

Draw leaves on the tree.

Color the sky blue.

Add other signs of spring.

Name _____

Mystery Picture

Cut out the box below. Then cut the puzzle pieces apart along the dashed lines and put the pieces together to make a bird picture. Glue them onto another sheet of paper. Color the picture.

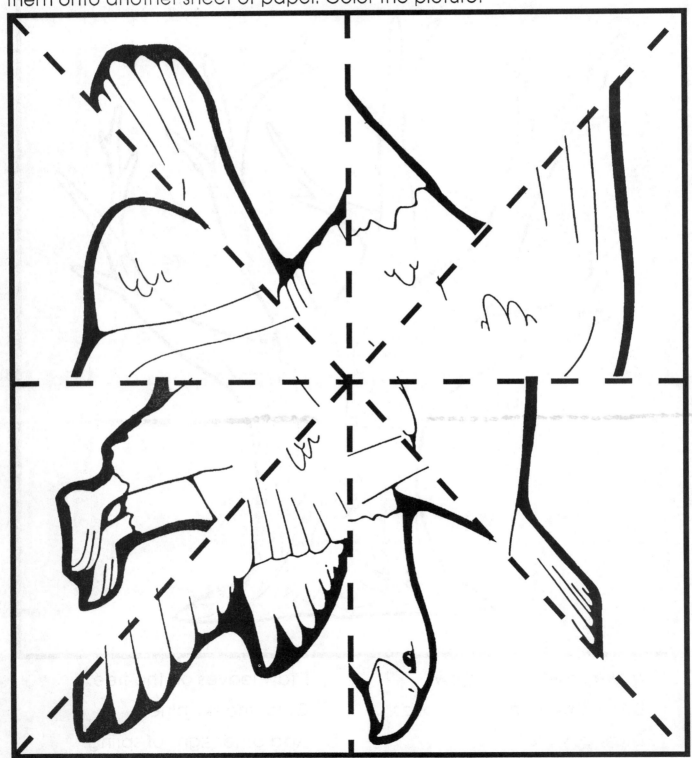

68

Owl Tear Art

*See activity 11 on page 9 for directions.

Nibble Nests

Imagine a nest you can really eat!

Follow this recipe and enjoy a "sweet tweet."

Ingredients:

1 jar (7 oz./210 g) marshmallow cream

1/2 cup (125 mL) creamy peanut butter

4 tablespoons (60 mL) butter (soft)

1 (8 ½ oz./250 g) can chow mein noodles

1 bag jelly bean "eggs"

butter for fingers

plastic wrap

Equipment:

muffin liners

measuring cups and spoons

medium size bowl

large spoon

Directions:

1. Mix marshmallow cream, peanut butter, and soft butter until blended well.

2. Add noodles and mix well.

3. Drop a large spoonful into a paper muffin liner. Shape into nests with greased fingers. Let stand until firm.

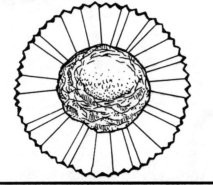

4. Fill with jelly bean "eggs." Enjoy in class or wrap to take home to share.

70

Readers' Theater Presentation

Set aside a day for presentation of "Chicken Licken." Invite parents or another class to enjoy the play. Send pop-up invitations (pages 71-72).

After the play, you may wish to distribute awards for completion of the unit and/or special activities and efforts made by students. Display bird folders, projects, experiments, and other across the curriculum activities completed during the unit.

Serving refreshments adds a festive touch to the day. Serve Nibble Nests (page 70) or bird shaped cookies and punch. Enjoy!

Pop-Up Invitation

Materials: 9" x 12" (23 cm x 30 cm) white construction paper (2 pieces per student); glue; crayons, colored pencils, or markers; scissors; copies of peacock (page 72)

1. Have students fold a piece of paper in half and cut a slit on the fold 3" (8 cm) in from each edge. Make slits about 2" (5 cm) long.

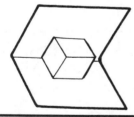

2. Open the fold, push it through, and crease it to form a pop-up section (see illustration).

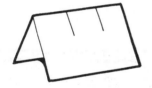

3. Fold the second piece of construction paper in half and glue it to the first as shown. (This becomes the front and back of the invitation.)

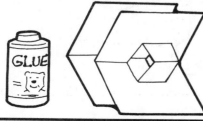

4. Work with students on the what, when, and where details and write these on the inside (top section) of the invitation.

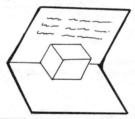

5. Color the peacock on page 72. Use vibrant colors for the plumage. Cut it out and glue it to the pop-up section (see illustration).

6. Glue on (and color, if desired) the front cover (top of page 72).

Pop-Up Invitation

72

Letters to Parents

Dear Parents,

We are beginning a whole language, thematic unit on birds. I would appreciate your help by allowing your child to bring items to school relating to this theme. Books, puppets, magazines, empty nests, feathers, and pictures will enrich our unit. Please label items with your child's name and expect it to be returned in about _____ weeks.

Thank you,

_____
Teacher's signature

✂ –

Dear Parents,

We will be making Nibble Nests at _____ on _____ and we need your help.

We would greatly appreciate it if _____ could ·bring in the following item(s):

_____

If you will be able to assist us in the classroom please check the box in the tear-off portion below.

Thank you,

_____
Teacher's signature

– –

Please tear off this portion and return it to school   by _____.
My child, _____, can bring in _____.

I will be able to help in class. ☐   _____
Parent's signature

Creating a Learning Center

A Learning Center is a special area set aside in the classroom for the study of a specific topic. Typically, a Learning Center contains a variety of activities and materials that teach, reinforce and enrich skills and concepts. Because students often learn in a variety of ways and at different rates, a Learning Center can be a valuable means of providing for these differences. Activities in a given center should be based on the abilities, needs, and interests of the students in your classroom. Learning Centers are equally appropriate for cooperative groups and individual use.

How to Create a Learning Center

- Select a theme or topic in any subject area (e.g., birds). Label the center attractively with a display or poster.
- Determine specific skills or concepts to be taught or reinforced (e.g., birds, nests, feathers, eggs).
- Develop appropriate learning activities (e.g., life cycle viewer, incubator, science experiments).
- Prepare extended activities for reinforcement or enrichment (e.g., worksheets, art activities binoculars, creative writing, chants, poems).
- Gather all materials needed to complete the projects at this center.

Scheduling Center Time

- Plan a rotating schedule where groups of children are rotated to different activities. For example, one group can be attending a teacher-directed lesson, while the second group completes seat work, and the third group is at the Learning Center.
- Assign individuals or small groups to the center according to diagnosed needs.
- Have a set center time each day. Assign a different group each day to work at the center during that time.

Record Keeping

- Make a monthly calendar for each student. Store it in a three-ring binder at the center. Record information in the appropriate spaces.
- Keep a file box with students' names listed alphabetically on index cards. Record notes and activities completed on the cards.

Bird Stationery

Bulletin Board

Whooo Knows?

What is the tallest bird alive today?

Which is the smallest bird?

Which bird is the fastest swimmer?

Which bird is our national bird?

Do all birds sing?

Can all birds fly?

Which bird lays the largest egg?

Objective

- This bulletin board may be used to introduce or reinforce the concepts learned during the bird unit. Adding students' work will make them feel good about themselves and point out how much they've learned.

Materials

- Background paper; construction paper; scissors; pushpins; stapler; sentence strips; students' work to be displayed; owl pattern (page 77)

Construction

- Reproduce and color the owl face on page 77. Put up the background paper. With push pins or staples, attach a heading, "Whooo Knows?," with the owl face placed above bulletin board (beak hanging over the edge).

Suggested Uses

1. To introduce the unit, gather students around the board and discuss each question briefly. Explain some of the activities in which they will be involved.

2. As an ongoing activity, make owl patterns from page 69 in which to display student responses to bulletin board questions. As a student researches the answers, write his/her name inside the owl pattern and the response. (For example, Jay knows that the hummingbird is the smallest bird.) Place students' owls around the bulletin board questions.

Owl Pattern for Bulletin Board

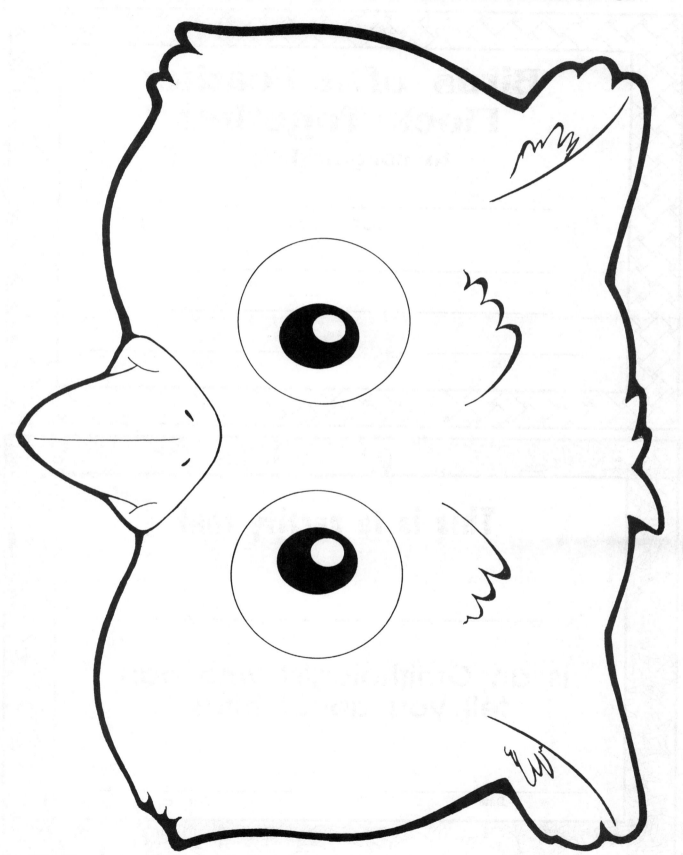

Awards

Birds of a Feather Flock Together
to congratulate

_____

for

_____

_____

_____   _____
Date   Teacher

This is to certify that

_____

is an Ornithologist who can tell you about birds.

_____   _____
Date   Teacher

Bibliography

Core Books

Ehlert, Lois. *Feathers For Lunch*. Harcourt Brace Jovanovich, 1990
Kellogg, Steven, retold by. *Chicken Little*. William Morrow and Co., 1985

Fiction

Brown, Margaret Wise. *The Golden Egg Book*. Golden Press, 1976
Butterworth, Oliver. *The Enormous Egg*. Atlantic Monthly Press, 1956
Eastman, P.D. *Are You My Mother?* Random House, 1967
Ellis, Anne Leo. *Dabble Duck*. Harper and Row Jr., 1987
Fox, Mem. *Hattie and the Fox*. Bradbury Press, 1988
Galdone, Paul. *Henny Penny*. Clarion, 1969
Galdone, Paul. *The Little Red Hen*. Clarion, 1979
Hutchins, Pat. *Rosie's Walk*. Macmillan, 1968
Lear, Edward. *Owl and the Pussycat*. Harper and Row, 1987
McCloskey, Robert. *Make Way for Ducklings*. Penguin, 1976
Oppenheim, Joanne. *Have You Seen Birds?* Scholastic, 1987
Polacco, Patricia. *Rechenka's Eggs*. Philomel Books, 1988
Seuss, Dr. *Horton Hatches the Egg*. Random House, 1940
Yolen, Jane. *Owl Moon*. Putnam Publishing Group, 1987

Nonfiction

Back, Christine and Olesn, J. *Chicken and Egg*. Silver Burdett Company, 1986
Burnie, David. *Bird*. Alfred A. Knopf, 1988
Caitlin, Stephen. *Amazing World of Birds*. Troll Associates, 1989
Gray, Ian. *Bird of Prey*. Mallard Press, 1990
Heller, Ruth. *Chickens Aren't the Only Ones*. Putnam Publishing Group, 1981
Heller, Ruth. *Many Luscious Lollipops: A Book About Adjectives*. Putnam, 1989
Minelli, Alessandro and Ruffo Sandro. *Great Book of Birds*. Random House, 1990
Robins, Chandler S. *A Guide to Field Identification of Birds of North America*. Golden Press, 1983
Selsam, Millicent. *A First Look at Bird Nests*. Walker and Co., 1984
Tyrrel, Esther. *Hummingbirds*. Crown, 1985

Music and Poetry

Glazer, Tom. *Tom Glazer's Treasury of Songs for Children*. Doubleday, 1988
Prelutsky, Jack, *The New Kid on the Block*. Greenwillow Books, 1984
Prelutsky, Jack (Sel. by). *The Random House Book of Poetry for Children*. Random House, 1983
Silverstein, Shel. *Where the Sidewalk Ends*. Harper and Row, 1974

Magazines

Your Big Backyard. National Wildlife Federation. 8925 Leesburg Pike, Vienna, VA 22184-0001
Zoobooks (Owls, Penguins, Birds of Prey, Geese and Swans, Parrots, etc.), P.O.Box 85271 Suite 6, San Diego, CA 92138

Teacher Created Materials

TCM 272 Thematic Unit- *Our Environment*
TCM 277 Thematic Unit-*Penguins*
TCM 342 *Connecting Math and Literature* (The Wolf's Chicken Stew)

Answer Key

Pages 11-13 (Bird Names)
1. Red-headed Woodpecker
2. Red-winged Blackbird
3. American Robin
4. Ruby-throated Hummingbird
5. American Goldfinch
6. House Sparrow
7. House Wren
8. Mourning Dove
9. Northern Oriole
10. Blue Jay
11. Northern Cardinal
12. Northern Flicker

Page 28
1. He plans to eat them. Foxy looks through recipe pages.
2. Answers will vary.
3. Chicken Little let panic overrule common sense. Answers will vary.
4. Foxy offered them a way to the palace, but had no intention of taking them there.
5. Chicken Little remembered the wanted poster of Foxy Loxy.
6. The acorn soared into the sky and hit the Sky Patrol helicopter propeller gears, causing it to crash into the poultry truck. Sergeant Hefty stopped the fleeing Foxy by flattening him. Foxy was sent to prison. Chicken Little recovered the acorn and planted it next to her house, where it grew into a huge oak tree.

Page 36
1. Chicken Little
2. Cocky Locky
3. Foxy Loxy
4. Goosey Lucy
5. Ducky Lucky
6. Turkey Lurkey

Page 38
duck egg = 2" (5 cm)
chicken egg = about 2 1/2" (6 cm)
hummingbird egg = between 1/2 and 1" (between 1 and 2 cm)
The chicken's egg was the longest.
The hummingbird's egg was the shortest.

Page 46
I have a pet parakeet. His name is Pretty Boy. He sits on my finger. Pretty Boy can talk. He says, "Hello, Pretty Boy." I'm teaching him more tricks. His favorite foods are: apples, sunflower seeds, potato chips, and lettuce. Would you like to have a pet parakeet? You can buy one at a pet store. Be sure to read a book about taking care of your bird.

Page 48
1. All birds lay eggs.
2. Do you watch birds?(You do watch birds.)
3. Some birds can talk. (Can some birds talk?)
4. Let's make a bird feeder.

Page 52
1. 12 in all
2. 21 in all
3. 5 left
4. 6 do not have worms
5. 25 left
6. 31 in all
7. 5 more
8. 4 eggs

Page 53
Message: Which came first, the chicken or the egg?
Code:

O = 1	I = 43	M = 87
H = 13	F = 21	R = 10
T = 33	G = 59	N = 64
W = 32	A = 35	S = 48
E = 29	C = 38	K = 65

Page 58
cwron = crown
ilbl = bill
btreas = breast
ginw = wing
gel = leg

yee = eye
nkee = knee
tali = tail
tofo = foot

Page 60

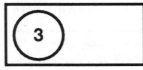
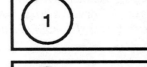
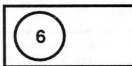
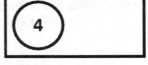

Page 68

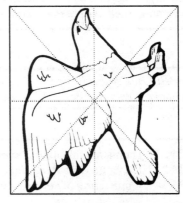